A Mob of Kangaroos

poems

Kip Knott

ISBN: 979-8-9914184-0-9

Ridge Books
www.eastridgereview.com

RIDGE
BOOKS

Table of Contents

There's a lullaby for suffering
And a paradox to blame
But it's written in the scriptures
And it's not some idle claim
You want it darker
We kill the flame

—Leonard Cohen, "You Want It Darker"

Tensile Strength

Washington D. C., January 6, 2021

The Kangaroo Court had begun work
on their gallows the night before. By dawn,

they were ready to carry out sentences.
No one knew for certain what would happen

if they succeeded, or how many bodies
might swing from the end of the noose,

or whether any rope could bear so much weight.

From Just the Right Angle

the Capitol rotunda fits perfectly
within the teardrop of the noose.

Fight Club: A Found Poem

excerpts taken from Donald Trump's speech on the morning of January 6, 2021

They're out there fighting.
The House guys are fighting.

And you have to get your people to fight.
And if they don't fight,

we have to primary the hell out of the ones that don't fight.
Republicans are constantly fighting.

I'd fight,
they'd fight,

I'd fight,
they'd fight.

But our fight
is just getting started. And we will fight.

And we're going to have to fight.
Now we're out here fighting.

We fight
like hell. And if you don't fight

like hell, you're not going to have a country anymore.

In a Crowd at the Capitol

after "In a Station of the Metro" by Ezra Pound

The bared teeth of these faces in the mob,
thorns on a frozen locust bough.

City on a Hill

"We've lost the line!"
—Capitol Police Officer, January 6, 2021

When the mob finally climbed the hill
and crossed over the Capitol threshold

wielding spears jerry-rigged
out of balustrades and flagpoles,

one can only wonder if America witnessed
its own kind of Rubicon. After all,

what is left to hang the American Dream on?

Indivisible

The horned Shaman gavels
the gathering to disorder

and delivers his sermon
"Death to tyrants!" beneath

the flags of two countries
the same, yet separate.

Both flags bear identical colors:
red, white, and blue—

one nation under mob rule.

A Brief History of Zip-Ties: A Found Poem

Eric Munchel was labeled "Zip-tie Guy" on January 6, 2021, after he was photographed running down a Senate chamber hallway holding dozens of the restraints.

According to *Wikipedia*, cable ties (more commonly known as zip-ties) were first manufactured in 1958 under the brand name Ty-Rap. Zip-ties are used as a type of fastener for holding items together. Because of their low cost, ease of use, and binding strength, zip-ties are used in a wide range of other applications. The most common zip-tie, normally made of nylon, has a flexible tape section with teeth that engage with a pawl in the head to form a ratchet so that as the free end is pulled, the zip-tie tightens and does not come undone. When the mouthpiece is inserted through the grooves and pulled tight, it creates a secure, adjustable loop, which locks in place like a knot. Stainless steel versions of zip-ties, some coated with a rugged plastic, may be used in hazardous environments under extreme conditions.

Outside the Halls

after "Between Walls" by William Carlos Williams

on the back steps
of the

Capitol where
insurrection

tried to grow lie
red puddles

in which shine
the broken

shards of bulletproof
glass

Original Sin

Our gravest sin is our belief
that America is a kind of Heaven

on earth, forgetting that Heaven
always begins with loss,

not enlightenment.

The Plunge

It's easy enough to step that one step forward and fall
endlessly away from the troubles that trouble the world
around me, around you, around us all.

To take that one step away from the edge and fall
back into all the divisions and ills that plague this world,
that step is the hardest step of all.

Whichever way I choose to move I know that I will fall
upon a high wire stretched between the precipice of a world
I will come to know all in all

and the precipice of a world that seems ready to fall.

Distress Signal

I turn off the TV and leave the ruins of America
behind as I walk through a deep winter night.

The only voices I hear now are the voices of crows
rioting against the cold, and the river's voice

trapped under ice. The snow couldn't care less
that it erases the Morse Code S.O.S. of my footprints

and the path that leads back home. Darkness wraps
around me like a straight-jacket until I cannot escape

the crows that tear the remnants of the world to shreds.

Hunted

Though the ashes still glow,
it has already begun: owls

suited to the dark silently hunt
the smoldering ruins of my despair.

Except for the light of their eyes,
they are invisible, like the new moon

feeding on a star-filled sky.

Cosmic Mycelium

We are made of starstuff.
— Carl Sagan

Even the fallow field surrounding my house
bears fruit every night when the moon rises—

either full of light or full of darkness
or not full of either—from some underworld

to claim its tract of sky, never free
of the invisible umbilical roots that bind it

to our planet, an earth-born yet unearthly
mushroom seeding the vast dark field

of the night with luminous spores that lie
dormant for a hundred-million lifetimes until,

inevitably, violently, they blossom into stars.

Hunters

Beneath wind and rain,
held in the dying arms

of the earth, something
wants free of the world.

I scour deep furrows
for arrowheads

and shards of pottery
that escaped dirt and plow.

Buzzards circle overhead.
Like me, they are also

hunting for the dead.

Mound City, Ohio

For a moment I feel another world pressing
through the ground just beneath my feet.

I call out, listening to the afterlife of my words
echo around me from one mound to the next,

dying a little with each repetition until all I can hear
is the whisper of something neither *Hello* nor *Goodbye*.

Nightly News

Bats rip the surface of the pond
for quick sips of water.

Feeding fish slice through
moonlight and limbs.

Fireflies ignite between
bloated and bursting cattails.

Tree frogs sizzle
in the dying, brittle willow.

I cannot escape
the violence of the night.

Deer Blind

The shadows of trees spread over the world.
I sit in the ribs of a sycamore next to the dry
tongue of Sunday Creek and watch for deer.

The moon climbs into its night-time blind
to hunt the cloudless dark for stars.
A screech owl settles on a branch above me,

freezing rabbits in the fallow field below.
Silo lights from surrounding farms blink on.
Thickets whisper the approach of deer.

Suddenly, distant gunshots pepper the air.

Spring Constellations

Uvalde, Texas, May 24, 2022

I used to believe in the spirit animals and gods
that I found in constellations of stars.
But when I look at the sky tonight, I see
only bullet holes piercing the dark,

one for every child we've lost, two for all
the children we will keep on losing
until constellations bleed together and the night
sky becomes something other than night,

something horribly empty and horribly full.

Lapsed

At ten years old I prayed
every night before I closed my eyes
that I would live a long life.

By twelve I had come to know death
was not the empty robin's nest
just outside my bedroom window,

but the desiccated hatchling
lying on the ground below
curled into itself forever.

Dyslexic Breakfast

The morning oatmeal and headlines coalesce
like a prosthetic ear grafted to a mouse's back.
On TV, the familiar sound of another mass shooting
erupts as a grackle crashes into the kitchen window
on a too windy day. Weather predictions
for hometowns past and present ticker-tape
across the screen: London's trite fog conceals
all traces of adolescent love; Fairbanks freezes
the skin of a live-in-lover; the rain in Waverly
glistens in the hair of infatuated students; damp
Columbus aggravates my ex-wife's asthma;
and all forecast a seventy-five percent chance
of regret. Stray bits of orange juice pulp dangle
from the rim of my glass like medals
on a general's starched dress coat.
Outside, where I wage my war with armies
of crab grass and dandelions, the cat carries
a robin under the rusting Christmas tree.
All summer the body count will mount,
but the dead will remain unidentified.
As the morning unfolds, CNN marks
the third anniversary of January 6, 2021
while a man in Ukraine whose ears were burned
off in the horrors of war waits patiently
until the mouse has heard enough.

After Another Mass Shooting

I find a puddle of sky on the sidewalk
and bow down to get a closer look.

A jet's contrail slices across the puddle
as if incising it for dissection.

Ants along the edge dip their pincers
in, microscopic ripples radiating

from all sides before colliding in the middle.
The sun appears from beneath a cloud just in time

to be snuffed out by the boot of a pedestrian
who couldn't care less whether

the world is right-side up or upside down.

Grief

A shadow stretches out on the pavement
only a few steps in front of me.
But this shadow does not belong to me.

This shadow belongs to a stray cloud
drifting in an otherwise cloudless sky.
The cloud floats too far away

for its shadow or me to reach, to touch,
but close enough to tear itself apart
on the spire of the cathedral towering over

what remains of both of us.

Terms of Venery

January 6, 2024

Three years later, the debate still rages:
peaceful protest or attempted insurrection?

Even what to call the group that ran wild
through the marble halls of the Capitol

has yet to be agreed upon:
A group of overzealous tourists

looking for the best patriotic selfie,
or a riotous gang of rebels?

But watching again members of the crowd
hopping fences and punching their way

past police lines and security guards,
all I see is a mob of kangaroos,

something absurd and ridiculous
with claws sharp enough to eviscerate.

An American Prayer

does not begin with faith
or a belief
in any Almighty.

It does not beseech
a God for love
or goodwill for anyone.

It does not appeal
for forgiveness
or beg for righteousness.

It does not call
for empathy, sympathy,
or unity of any kind.

If we learned anything
from January 6, 2021,
we learned this:

the real American
prayer begins with "I want"
and moves on to

"damn everyone else"
and never ends with
"Go in peace."

Acknowledgments

ONE ART: "Lapsed," "The Plunge," "Spring Constellations"
The Potomac: "Dyslexic Breakfast"
Seasonal Fruits: "Cosmic Mycelium"
tiny wren lit: "After Another Mass Shooting," "Grief," "The Plunge"

About the Author

Kip Knott is a 7th generation Appalachian who was born and raised in Ohio. Over the years, he has called England, Alaska, Michigan, Iowa, and Oklahoma home. In 2001, he found his way back to Ohio, where he has lived ever since. He is the author of eight previous poetry chapbooks and three full-length collections of poetry, the most recent being *The Other Side of Who I Am* (Kelsay Books, 2023). His first full-length collection of stories, *Some Birds Nest in Broken Branches*, was published in 2021 by Alien Buddha Press. His writing and photography have appeared in *Barren*, *Beloit Fiction Journal*, *Best Microfiction 2024*, *Gettysburg Review*, *The Greensboro Review*, *ONE ART*, *Poet Lore*, *The Sun*, *Virginia Quarterly Review*, and *Wigleaf Top 50*. His writing has been nominated for Best of the Net and Pushcart prizes, and he is the recipient of grants from the Ohio Arts Council for both poetry and playwriting. Currently, he is a teacher, photographer, and part-time art dealer who spends his free time traveling throughout Appalachia and the Midwest taking photographs and searching for lost art treasures.

www.ingramcontent.com/pod-product-compliance
Lightning Source LLC
Chambersburg PA
CBHW051742040426
42447CB00008B/1265